I0516981

SUSANNE JORN

*Andalusiske øjebliksbilleder
i november*

Andalusian Snapshots
in November

*Translated from the Danish by
David McDuff*

SPUYTEN DUYVIL

New York City

© 2022 Susanne Jorn
Translation © 2022 David McDuff
Asger Jorn: *Mit slot i Spanien (My Castle in Spain)*, 1954, oil on masonite, 122 x 91, 5 cm,
SMK - National Gallery of Denmark, © Donation Jorn / VISDA
SMK Photo: Jakob Skou-Hansen.
ISBN 978-1-956005-83-7

Original Danish title: Andalusiske øjebliksbilleder i november. Photographs by Steen Møller
Rasmussen. Forlaget Lundtofte. Kgs. Lyngby, 2010.

Library of Congress Cataloging-in-Publication Data

Names: Jorn, Susanne, author. | McDuff, David, 1945- translator. | Jorn,
    Susanne. Andalusiske øjebliksbilleder i november. | Jorn, Susanne.
    Andalusiske øjebliksbilleder i november. English.
Title: Andalusiske øjebliksbilleder i november = Andalusian Snapshots in
    November / Susanne Jorn ; translated from the Danish by David McDuff.
Other titles: Andalusian Snapshots in November
Description: New York City : Spuyten Duyvil, [2022] | Danish text with
    parallel English translation on facing pages.
Identifiers: LCCN 2022026652 | ISBN 9781956005837 (paperback)
Subjects: LCGFT: Poetry.
Classification: LCC PT8176.22.Y56 A8513 2022 | DDC
    839.811/74--dc23/eng/20220608
LC record available at https://lccn.loc.gov/2022026652

simple
poetry
lives
in spite of everything,
has an eternity that is not afraid

Pablo Neruda – 'Ode to Envy'
Elemental Odes, 1954

CONTENTS

Spilkogende novembersol
Broiling November sun

VINDSTILLE
NO WIND

Stilhedens
The silence's

Stilhedens
The silence's

Middelhavets
The Mediterranean's

Synger cikader mon i kor
Do cicadas sing in chorus

Den trommehindesprængende blæst her i natørkenen
The eardrum-splitting gale here in the nocturnal desert

Jeg
I

MIN INDRE ZONE
MY INNER ZONE

ET GRANATÆBLE
A POMEGRANATE

Underdejligste granatæbletræ
Most wonderfully lovely pomegranate tree

Det siges
It is said

Granada er stedet
Granada is the place

SIESTA
SIESTA

I endeløse, dybe minutter
In endless deep minutes

LET BRISE
LIGHT BREEZE

Bjergsti
Mountain path

TORDENBLÅ SKYBJERGE
THUNDER-BLUE CLOUD MOUNTAINS

Grønne Lykkedrager sover
Green Lucky Dragons sleep

Den liljehvide passionsdigter
That lily-white poet of passion

HVIDKALKET MUR
WHITEWASHED WALL

EVIGBLÅ
ETERNAL BLUE

STANK
STENCH

Alkoholikerens
The alcoholic's

HVID BRÆGEN
WHITE BLEATING

Hyrder
Shepherds

HVID HEJRE
WHITE HERON

Sierra Cabrera bjergene
The mountains of Sierra Cabrera

FARVEMAGIEN
THE COLOUR-MAGIC

Som himmeltæpper
Like celestial carpets

Andalusiske øjebliksbilleder

i november

Andalusian Snapshots

in November

Spilkogende novembersol
og gule, røde, brune, sorte
jordfarver overalt
i Eras del Lugar dalen.

Fra mørkt sind
til lyst sind.

Pastelgul Lysfølsomhed.

Broiling November sun
and yellow, red, brown, black
earth colours everywhere
in Eras del Lugar valley.

From dark mood
to light mood.

Pastel yellow Photosensitivity

VINDSTILLE

STORMÆGTIGT
PASTELBLÅT LYS

NO WIND

MAGNIFICENT
PASTEL-BLUE LIGHT

Stilhedens
puls slår
mens den fortryllende
Eras del Lugar dal
klinger papirhvidt
i Intethedens
totale tomhed.

Stilhedens
puls slår...

The silence's
pulse throbs
while the enchanting
Eras del Lugar valley
chimes paper-white
in the total blankness
of Nothing.

The silence's
pulse throbs...

Stilhedens
Altseende
Undtagelses-
tilstand.

Skorpionens
sære
tavshed.

The silence's
All-seeing
State of
Emergency.

The scorpion's
weird
muteness.

Middelhavets
dybazurblå,
Middelhavets
lyseazurblå

Piedra de Villazar strandens
gulbrune sand
Piedra de Villazar strandens
grovkornede sandskorn og

blækblå sjælefred.

The Mediterranean's
deep azure,
the Mediterranean's
light azure

The yellow-brown sand
of Piedra de Vilazar beach
the coarse-grained sand
of Piedra de Vilazar beach and

my ink-blue peace of mind.

Synger cikader mon i kor
ved mørkets komme.

Synger fårekyllinger mon i kor
ved mørkets komme.

Nej, de synger om kap
i andalusiske aftenlydmure.

Do cicadas sing in chorus
as darkness arrives.

Do crickets sing in chorus
as darkness arrives.

No, they compete at singing
in Andalusian eveningsoundwalls.

Den trommehindesprængende blæst her i natørkenen
minder mig om dengang jeg var så vred på det hele.

Ingenting skulle der til, og jeg sprang i luften
så mine vredessatellitter tindrede på alle himlene.

Skodderne slår mod husmurene. Fjerne stjerner lyser på
ørkenhimlen. I horisonten blinker en lille vredessatellit vist.

That eardrum-splitting gale here in the nocturnal desert
reminds me of way back when I was so angry about everything.

There was no way round it, and I leapt in the air
so my anger-satellites sparkled in all the heavens.

The shutters flap against the house walls. Distant stars shine in
the desert sky. On the horizon I think a little anger-satellite is blinking.

Jeg
Nåede
Aldrig
Op
Til
Toppen
Af
Det
Hellige
Bjerg.
Jeg
Gik
Næsten
Hele
Vejen
Op
På
Montem
Sacrum.
Jeg
Nåede
Mere
End
Halvvejen
Op
På
Mojácar
La
Vieja,
Som
Pyramidebjerget
Også
Hedder.

I
Never
Got
Up
To
The
Top
Of
The
Holy
Mountain.
I
Walked
Almost
The
Whole
Way
Up
Montem
Sacrum.
I
Got
More
Than
Halfway
Up
Mojácar
La
Vieja,
As
The
Pyramid
Mountain
Is
Also
Called.

MIN INDRE ZONE -
HALVMÅNEN
OVER MOJÁCAR

MY INNER ZONE -
THE HALF MOON
OVER MOJÁCAR

ET GRANATÆBLE
EN NÆLDENS TAKVINGE
ET GRANATÆBLE

A POMEGRANATE
A SMALL TORTOISESHELL
A POMEGRANATE

Underdejligste granatæbletræ.
Underskønneste granatæble.
Kærlighedens granatæblerøde frugt.

Ikke andet.

Most wonderfully lovely pomegranate tree.
Most wonderfully beautiful pomegranate.
Love's pomegranate-red fruit.

Nothing else.

Det siges
at granatæbler
renser kroppen
for had og jalousi.

Hvis det siges
at poesien
er sjælens åndedræt,
må granatæbler
være kærlighedsdigte
alle sammen.

It is said
that pomegranates
cleanse the body
of hatred and jealousy.

If it is said
that poetry
is the breath of the soul
then pomegranates must
be love poems
all together.

Granada er stedet,
hvor mange granatæbletræer vokser.
Granada er stedet,
hvor paladset Alhambra ligger.

Jeg for vild i Alhambra.
Og
stod pludselig
i Alhambras hemmelige sal.

I et hjørne af salen kunne jeg mærke
nærværet af en mand i det tætte mørke.

Jeg satte mig i salens modsatte hjørne
og hviskede min hemmelighed til ham.

Først da
kunne jeg
fortsætte ad
den skæbnebestemte vej.

Granada is the place
where many pomegranate trees grow.
Granada is the place
where the Alhambra palace is.

I got lost in the Alhambra.
Lost,
I suddenly stood
in the Alhambra's secret chamber.

In one corner of the chamber I could sense
the presence of a man in the thick darkness.

I sat down in the chamber's opposite corner
and whispered my secret to him.

Only then
could I
continue along
my fate-determined road.

SIESTA
RUNDSAV
SIESTA

SIESTA
CIRCULAR SAW
SIESTA

I endeløse, dybe minutter
af penetrabel transparens
forenes jeg med mine digte i koaner

mens
to tuschsorte dagugleøjne
bare
stirrer og stirrer og stirrer
gådefuldt
durk igennem mig.

In endless deep minutes
of penetrable transparency
I unite with my poems in koans

while
two ink-black daytime-owl-eyes
just
stare and stare and stare
mysteriously
right through me

LET BRISE –
MUSIKKEN
I TØRT PAMPASGRÆS

LIGHT BREEZE -
THE MUSIC
IN DRY PAMPAS GRASS

Bjergsti
Trillingranker
Pyramidepopler

Bjergsti
Appelsinlund
Figenkaktus

Bjergsti
Rosmarin
Passionsblomst.

Mountain path
Bougainvillea
Balsam poplars

Mountain path
Orange grove
Barbary fig

Mountain path
Rosemary
Passion flower.

TORDENBLÅ SKYBJERGE
DRØMMEBROER
DISHVIDE SKYDALE

THUNDER-BLUE CLOUD MOUNTAINS
DREAM BRIDGES
MIST-WHITE CLOUD VALLEYS

Grønne Lykkedrager sover
i Francisco Goya bjergenes grotter
og brummeknurrenynnesynge snorkelyde
høres langt væk og tæt på... I dag
så jeg vilde magiske øjne i fjerskyer,
et sjældent syn i november.

Green Lucky Dragons sleep
in the caves of Francisco Goya's mountains
and grumblemumblehummingsinging sounds of snoring
can be heard far away and away... Today
I saw wild magic eyes in feather-clouds,
a rare sight in November.

Den liljehvide passionsdigter
Nej, den ceruleanblå håbdigter
Flammerøde ikke-volddigter
Natsorte tolerancedigter
Erik Stinus -
er død 13.11.2009.

That lily-white poet of passion
No, that cerulean blue poet of hope
Flame red poet of non-violence
Night black poet of tolerance
Erik Stinus –
died on 13.11.2009.

HVIDKALKET MUR
EN GEKKO
EN PALIMPSEST

WHITEWASHED WALL
ONE GECKO
ONE PALIMPSEST

EVIGBLÅ
STRANDKANTSMUSIK -

MIDDELHAVSBØLGERNE

ETERNAL BLUE
SEASHORE MUSIC –

THE MEDITERRANEAN WAVES

STANK
AF BRÆNDT BILDÆK

NABOENS BAGHAVEBÅL

STENCH
OF BURNT CAR TYRES

THE NEIGHBOUR'S BACKYARD BONFIRE

Alkoholikerens
tomme flasker
smidt ned
af en bjergskråning:
La hora de la verdad.

The alcoholic's
empty bottles
hurled down
from a mountain slope:
La hora de la verdad.

HVID BRÆGEN
SORT BRÆGEN

SORT/HVID BEVÆGELSE

WHITE BLEATING
BLACK BLEATING

BLACK/WHITE MOVEMENT

Hyrder
og
hyrdehund.

Hvide
får,
sorte
geder.

Hyrde
og
hyrdehunde.

Gulligt-
hvirvlende
støv.

Shepherds
and
sheepdog.

White
sheep,
black
goats.

Shepherds
and
sheepdogs.

Yellowish-
whirling
dust.

HVID HEJRE
PÅ FÅRERYG -

KUN LIDT

WHITE HERON
ON SHEEP'S BACK –

JUST A LITTLE BIT

Sierra Cabrera bjergene
vågner
i morgendisen.

Titusind diamanter
blinker
på Agua floden

denne
hvidmalede
morgen

med
hvid
magi
i.

The mountains of Sierra Cabrera
awake
in the morning mist.

Ten thousand diamonds
flash
on the River Agua

this
white-painted
morning

of
white
magic.

FARVEMAGIEN
I MIT INDRE MORGENGRY

OKKERGUL PASSION

THE COLOUR-MAGIC
IN MY INNER DAYBREAK

OCHRE-YELLOW PASSION

Som himmeltæpper
af stjerner,
drømme.

Som mure
af cypresser,
håb.

Som mure
af figentræer,
længsel.

Som mure
af appelsintræer,
livsglæde.

Som mure
af granatæbletræer,
medmenneskelighed.

Som mure
af oliventræer,
verdensfred.

Som skærme
med digte,
klang.

Som hærfuglen
mod ruden,
milepæle.

Like celestial carpets
of stars,
dreams.

Like walls
of cypresses,
hope.

Like walls
of fig trees,
longing.

Like walls
of orange trees,
joie de vivre.

Like walls
of pomegranate trees,
humanity.

Like walls
of olive trees,
universal peace.

Like screens
of poems,
sound.

Like the hoopoe
at the windowpane,
milestones.

Photo: Lærke Posselt

SUSANNE JORN has a masters in sinology, a masters in American literature and a Comprehensives for a Ph.D. in Comparative Literature.

The same year as her debut in the Danish poetry magazine *Hvedekorn* (1970) and while she was in Japan on a Monbusho grant (1969-1971), Susanne's debut poetry collection, *the splinters*, was released in Denmark. In 1971, she moved to the United States and has since travelled to Japan many times.

From 1970 to 1988 she used the name Susanne Lyngborg as an alias for her work as a writer and literary translator, and since 1988 she has been known by the name Susanne Jorn, starting with the publication of her fairy tale collection *The Dancing Donkey*.

Her work is heavily inspired by Chinese and Japanese poetry traditions and her many years in the US and Japan.

The influence from visual art is significant, especially in her use of color.

Many of her books are illustrated by visual artists such as Pierre Alechinsky, Carl-Henning Pedersen, Asger Jorn, Yasse Tabuchi, Yoshio Nakajima and Gao Xingjian. Conversely, Susanne has written poems and fairy tales to the work of visual artists. The latest example of this is *The Bird in the Forest* from 2014, featuring 53 poems and fairy tales to the works by 26 artists from the Museum Jorn Collection.

In *Passion Cycle* she wrote linked poetry (renshi) with the Japanese poet Hajime Kijima.

Susanne has translated several poetry collections from the Chinese and the Japanese to Danish. The most famous are Shuntaro Tanikawa, Kazuko Shiraishi, Hanshan and Yang Lian.

In 2018, Susanne was the recipient of The Drachmann Award. Her poems have been translated into eight different languages. The latest selection of her poems is: *Linedanserfarver / Couleurs funambules: Poèmes traduit du danois par Christine Berlioz et Laila Flink Thullesen*. Illustrations by Gao Xingjian. CD by Susanne Jorn and harp player Helen Davies. Éditions Grèges, 2018.

After moving to Copenhagen, Denmark in 2000 and while continuing to write and translate poetry, Susanne has worked with a series of Scandinavian composers and musicians. Since 2009, she has performed live with Celtic harp player Helen Davies while reading a selection from newly published books.

About the Translator

DAVID McDUFF is a literary translator and
critic. His translations of Nordic poetry
are published by Bloodaxe Books, U.K.,
and his translations of nineteenth and
twentieth century Russian prose fiction are
published in Penguin Classics.

www.ingramcontent.com/pod-product-compliance
Lightning Source LLC
Chambersburg PA
CBHW031229120626
46545CB00003B/1043